Bristol &

A DOG WALKER'S GUIDE

Nigel Vile

COUNTRYSIDE BOOKS
NEWBURY BERKSHIRE

First published 2012
Reprinted 2016, 2019, 2021
© Nigel Vile 2012

COUNTRYSIDE BOOKS
3 Catherine Road
Newbury, Berkshire

To view our complete range of books,
please visit us at
www.countrysidebooks.co.uk

ISBN 978 1 84674 293 4

Photographs by the author

Designed by Peter Davies, Nautilus Design
Produced through The Letterworks Ltd., Reading
Typeset by Jean Cussons Typesetting, Diss, Norfolk
Printed by The Holywell Press, Oxford

Contents

Walk

Appendix

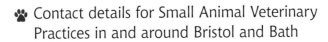

Area map showing location of the walks.

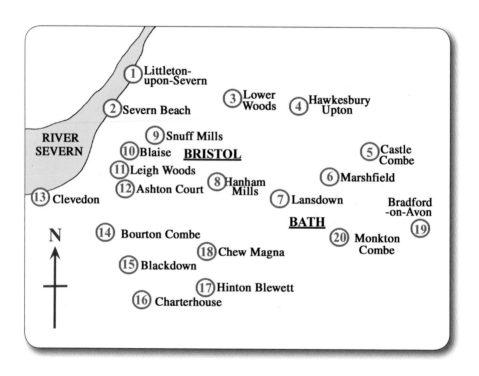

INTRODUCTION

I **have to confess to** having started off as something of a reluctant dog walker – in fact there was even a touch of antipathy towards man's best friend. In a former life, I was always a 'dog free' walker with many a walk being spoiled by thoughtless and careless dog owners. Uncontrolled dogs would come bounding across fields and along woodland paths, barking away and jumping all over the place with their muddy paws. There was even one occasion when a small group of large dogs quite literally knocked over one of my young children, instilling a genuine fear in what was at the time a three year old. The retort was nearly always that 'he's really friendly and is only playing'. And then there was dog excrement, either left on public rights of way or – perhaps even more cynically – picked up in one of those scented bags and left tied to a nearby branch.

Things changed in 2008 with the birth of my first grandchild. Finn, the family Jack Russell, suddenly found that he was no longer the number one attraction and quite often a walk consisted of little more than a snatched stroll in a nearby park. For a Jack Russell with its love of the great outdoors this must have seemed like purgatory – so in stepped grandfather to fill the occasional void. At first, it was hard work. Finn was little more than a young puppy and, given the chance to run free, could quite literally disappear. With a little training and the passage of time, however, he has become a lot more sensible and well behaved, the only exception being when his adopted owner arrives at the house. Such is his excitement, he engages in what can only be described as an outbreak of vertical jumping at the patio doors.

It soon became apparent that choosing a walk for a dog involved special considerations. Roads and traffic, for example were to be avoided if at all possible, as were fields where frisky livestock or sheep and lambs were to be found. Even a slim and agile Jack Russell could find the occasional stile akin to an obstacle course, adding yet another factor to the equation. And then there were the positives to include. Most dogs love chasing sticks, which makes a section of woodland along the way particularly attractive. Woods are also full of exciting scents and sounds, further adding to their appeal. Water is another attraction, and not only for drinking. Finn enjoys nothing more than quite literally diving into a river or pond in the style of Tom Daley to retrieve a stick, often being an amusing sideshow for passing walkers. A pub garden that welcomes dogs is always a must at journey's end, a place to rest and linger awhile at the end of a pleasant few hours in the great outdoors.

This collection of walks in the Bath and Bristol area has been devised with all these factors in mind. Where there are sections of road walking, they are generally on very quiet country lanes where the chance of meeting vehicles is minimal. If there are stiles, they are those with enough headway and clearance for all but the largest or most immobile dogs to pass through. In such cases, an alternative 'there-and-back' route has been suggested to ensure a decent walk nevertheless. There are woodland walks at Bourton Combe and Lower Woods, stretches of coastal path at Clevedon and Littleton-upon-Severn, riverside paths at Chew Magna and Snuff Mills, as well as open swathes of countryside at Hawkesbury Upton and Blackdown on the Mendip Hills. With landscape that includes limestone upland and river estuary, parkland and wooded valleys, there is something here for every dog and its owner.

Nigel Vile

....

PUBLISHER'S NOTE

We hope that you obtain considerable enjoyment from this book; great care has been taken in its preparation. Although at the time of publication all routes followed public rights of way or permitted paths, diversion orders can be made and permissions withdrawn.

We cannot, of course, be held responsible for such diversion orders and any inaccuracies in the text which result from these or any other changes to the routes, nor any damage which might result from walkers trespassing on private property. We are anxious though that all details covering the walks are kept up to date and would therefore welcome information from readers which would be relevant to future editions.

The simple sketch maps that accompany the walks in this book are based on notes made by the author whilst checking out the routes on the ground. They are designed to show you how to reach the start, to point out the main features of the overall circuit and they contain a progression of numbers that relate to the paragraphs of the text.

However, for the benefit of a proper map, we do recommend that you purchase the relevant Ordnance Survey sheet covering your walk. The Ordnance Survey maps are widely available, especially through booksellers and local newsagents.

ADVICE FOR DOG WALKERS

With open access to the countryside having become something of an issue in recent years, dog owners have to realise that with rights come obvious responsibilities. To quote from an official source 'the countryside is a great place to exercise dogs but it is every owner's duty to make sure their dog is not a danger or nuisance to farm animals, wildlife or other people'. With this in mind, a few gentle reminders:

- Ground nesting birds can often be found on the Mendip Hills between March and July. Be wary of letting your dog run free in the area at this time. Equally, pheasants are often released in large numbers into woodland in the early autumn. Notices requesting that dogs be kept on a lead at this time should obviously be respected.
- Sheep and lambs are by nature nervous creatures. As they turn and run, many dogs find it good fun to give chase. Such behaviour could cause a pregnant ewe to abort so signs warning that dogs worrying sheep could be shot are not there for fun. Lambing time, incidentally, is between January and March.
- Cattle are more often than not simply inquisitive rather than aggressive. A cow who considers her calf to be threatened in some way, however, is a different matter. The stories about walkers being injured by rampaging cows usually involve both calves and dogs. In such cases, the advice is to drop the dog lead and leave the dog to sort itself out. It is safer for both you and the dog.
- There may well be horses along the way on some of these walks, including wild ponies on Blackdown on the Mendip Hills. Horses tend to be very relaxed about both humans and dogs, usually completely ignoring their presence.
- The official source states that it is every dog owner's duty to make sure their dog is not a danger to other people. With this in mind, it goes without saying that any excrement is dealt with properly, and that your dog is not allowed to randomly jump up on other walkers enjoying a few hours in the countryside.

Enough of this necessary 'health and safety' detail, the majority of which is simple common sense and courtesy. With minimal road walking, few stiles and livestock at a minimum, these are a series of walks that I hope both you and your dog will very much enjoy. I wish you many hours of fun and relaxation walking in the countryside around Bath and Bristol.

1

Littleton-upon-Severn

Whale Wharf, near the start of the walk.

Although a little way from the river, Littleton would literally have been 'on-Severn' in centuries past when floods frequently swamped the local low-lying land. Drainage ditches and flood defences mean that the threat of flooding is no more, although the mighty Severn is some sight when first glimpsed as visitors crest those defences. The Severn rises on

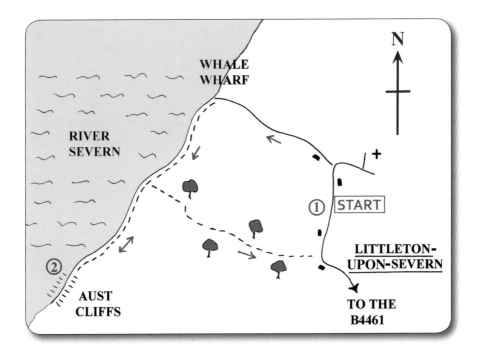

the eastern slopes of Plynlimmon, deep in Central Wales, from where its 210-mile journey to the Bristol Channel commences. Here the river is very much tidal, with the mud flats supporting large numbers of birds that are adapted to feed on the abundant supply of small, mud-dwelling creatures. Waders, such as the Dunlin, are especially common during the winter months. Lists of species to spot would be futile with so much depending upon the tides and the seasons, so simply come armed with your binoculars and bird-spotting books!

Other features along the way are Whale Wharf and Aust Cliffs. Once a tiny port importing Welsh coal and exporting local bricks, Whale Wharf is so named because in 1885 a whale was indeed stranded here on the outgoing tide. Today it is little more than a muddy inlet. The famous red and white cliffs at Aust are a landmark when crossing the original Severn Bridge into England. The site is a magnet for fossil collectors with 'a highly productive bone bearing bed at the very top from the Rhaetian Penarth series'. The bed is full of teeth, reptile and fish remains with the occasional rock fall meaning that fossils can be found along the foreshore.

Along the Severn's foreshore is all manner of debris left by the ebb and flow of tides. Included amongst the flotsam and jetsam is a good deal of driftwood

Dog factors

Distance: 4½ miles including the walk along to Aust Cliffs.
Road walking: A quiet ¾-mile cul de sac at the beginning. To avoid any road walking, simply drive to the car park at the end of this lane, just below the Severn, and do a there-and-back walk (3 miles in total) along the river to Aust Cliffs.
Livestock: Occasionally grazing by the Severn. Cattle here are used to dogs as this is a popular dog-walking area. If there are sheep grazing, then dogs should be kept under control.
Stiles: None.
Nearest vets: The Rowe Veterinary Group have a branch in Thornbury. ☎ 01454 415478.

that will provide perfect fodder for dogs who like chasing and retrieving sticks. The quiet track leading back to Littleton-upon-Severn from the river is quite the perfect place for dogs to run free and sniff out the smells of rabbits and maybe foxes or badgers.

Terrain

A flat and easy walk by the Severn. If you extend the walk beneath Aust Cliffs, there is some relatively rough walking along the foreshore.

Where to park

The roadside in Littleton-upon-Severn by the White Hart Inn – or park in the pub's car park (with permission) if you plan to eat and drink there either before or after the walk (GR ST 597901). **OS map:** Explorer 167 Thornbury, Dursley & Yate.

How to get there

Leave the M48 at junction 1 and follow the B4461 towards Alveston and Thornbury. In 2 miles, turn left along an unclassified road signposted to Littleton. The White Hart is on the right in the centre of the village.

Nearest refreshments

The White Hart is an excellent pub owned by Young's Brewery. In front of the inn is a large garden with dozens of picnic tables where dogs are most welcome. ☎ 01454 412275.

The Walk

. . . .

① With your back to the **White Hart**, follow the road to the right for 200 yards to a junction. Turn left and follow a quiet cul de sac lane waymarked to **Whale Wharf** for ¾ mile to a parking area. Pass through a handgate on the left to join a grassy bank – a flood barrier – alongside Whale Wharf and the **Severn Estuary**. Follow this bank towards the First Severn Crossing. In 600 yards, look out for a gate and path below the bank on the left – remember this point as it marks the return to Littleton. Continue following the bank for ¾ mile to a sewage works on the left. For an optional extension, follow the rough foreshore beneath **Aust Cliffs** along towards the First Severn Crossing.

② At some point, turn around and retrace your steps back to that gate and the path leading back to Littleton. Coming from the opposite direction, it will be below on the right. Pass through that handgate and cross a footbridge before following the left edge of a field up to a track in its top left corner. Follow this track – early on it bears right and left – for ¾ mile back to the road in **Littleton**. Turn left back to the **White Hart**.

The rugged Aust Cliffs.

2

Severn Beach

Swans enjoying some solitude.

River estuaries are magical places, places where fresh water meets the sea and where, at low tide, huge expanses of mudflats provide a happy hunting ground for thousands of wading birds. The Severn Estuary is no exception. At Severn Beach, which never quite took off as Bristol's 'Blackpool' when a railway link from the city was opened in the 19th century, the expansive views extend across the mudflats towards South Wales and the Forest of Dean. The outlook, however, is dominated by the Second Severn Crossing, built between 1992 and 1996 to relieve the pressure on the ageing original Severn Bridge. North of Severn Beach is New Passage, where a truncated pier marks the site of the terminus of the former South Wales Union Railway. It was from here that passengers – including the Wesleys in their quest to convert Wales – would disembark for the ferry to Portskewett across the water. Today, rail travellers have the simple, if less exciting, passage through the Severn Tunnel.

Dogs will love the traffic-free run along the promenade, as well as exploring the foreshore with its drift wood and other tide-line debris. This is popular dog-walking country, too, with the sights and smells of other dogs certain to appeal.

Terrain

A level walk along the Severn that essentially follows the riverside promenade with options to also walk along the river's foreshore.

Where to park

Station Road in Severn Beach (GR ST 540848). **OS map:** Explorer 154 Bristol West & Portishead or 167 Thornbury, Dursley & Yate.

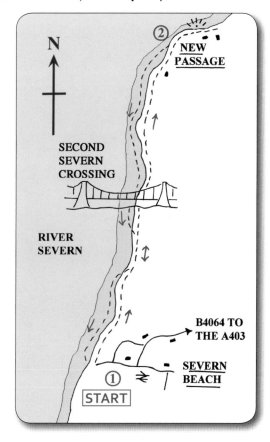

How to get there

Follow the A403 south from the M48 (junction 1) towards Avonmouth for 5 miles, before turning right on the B4064 towards Severn Beach. In ½ mile, bear left into Station Road and park on the roadside in the vicinity of the station.

Nearest refreshments

Downs Bakery in Beach Road at Severn Beach has a small café area, although dogs would have to stay outside. A better option is to take a picnic to enjoy from a seat with a view at New Passage.

The Walk

. . . .

1 At the end of **Station Road**, walk up to the Promenade, turn right and walk along to

Dog factors

Distance: 2 miles (can be extended to 4 miles – see directions).
Road walking: None.
Livestock: None.
Stiles: None.
Nearest vets: Viking Vets in Henbury. ☎ 0117 950 5888.

The view from the foreshore.

Fishing from the Severn Beach.

the **Second Severn Crossing**. Continue for another ¼ mile to a truncated pier on the left that marks the remains of the pier at **New Passage**. Continue for another 100 yards to a seat with a view north towards the **First Severn Crossing**. Retrace your steps back to the truncated pier and, in a few paces, veer right onto a lower level path that borders the shoreline.

(2) Follow this path until it rejoins the **Promenade** just past the **Second Severn Crossing**. Follow the Promenade for 150 yards until, just past a radar station, veer right onto another lower level path, which borders the shoreline. In 300 yards, rejoin the Promenade and follow its course back to **Station Road** – or alternatively, follow the rough shoreline back to the same point, tide permitting!

Footnote: At the end of the walk, it is possible to continue in a southerly direction along the foreshore towards Avonmouth for approximately 1 mile. There is a public right of way but, again, it would have to be a there-and-back linear walk.

Lower Woods

Lower Woods –paradise for dogs!

Woodlands, with their secretive glades, are magical places, and Lower Woods is no exception. Deer are frequent visitors to the rides and tracks although they are extremely timid creatures so spotting them does take a lot of time and patience! Spring is an excellent time to come down to the woods, with so many wild flowers carpeting the ground. Wood anemones and celandines, primroses and bluebells are but the most common species to look out for. And something rather special lives here – the nightingale. This elusive bird can be heard from the dense scrub along the woodland edge for just a few weeks around late April. However, you will have to be in the woodland either at dawn or dusk to enjoy the magnificent

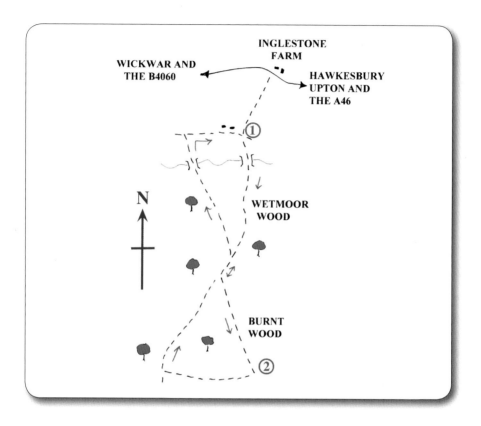

chorus that this fine creature produces. If you are very lucky, you could hear up to 20 birds in full song.

Dogs will absolutely love Lower Woods with its open rides and lack of stiles, traffic and livestock. There are sticks aplenty, plus all the sounds and smells of woodland. There is also the Little Avon River flowing through the heart of the wood. A relatively shallow and gently flowing stream, this is perfect for water-loving dogs to splash around in.

Terrain

The woodland paths are generally well defined, although potentially rutted and muddy in places. Signage is poor in the woods and, with side turns all over the place, it isn't difficult to get lost. This is no problem, however, as dogs will be quite happy strolling around in Lower Woods all day long ... and eventually you will find your way back to 'Horton Great Trench' as the main ride is known.

Dog factors
· ·

Distance: 2½ miles.
Road walking: None.
Livestock: None.
Stiles: None.
Nearest vets: Animal House Vets in Chipping Sodbury.
☎ 0117 3355999.

Where to park

The free public car park at Lower Woods by Lower Woods Lodge (GR ST 747881). **OS map:** Explorer 167 Thornbury, Dursley & Yate.

How to get there

A minor road runs cross country from the B4060 at Wickwar to Hawkesbury Upton. Midway between these two settlements, the lane crosses Inglestone Common. Opposite Inglestone Farm, follow a gravelled track into Lower Woods to reach the car park. There is no signage pointing the way to the car park.

Nearest refreshments

The Buthay in Wickwar (☎ 01454 299083) and the Beaufort Arms at Hawkesbury Upton (☎ 01454 238217) are the nearest pubs to Lower Woods. Both are traditional country pubs with gardens where dogs can relax whilst their owners enjoy delicious home-made food and a selection of real ales.

The Walk
· ·

1 At the entrance to **Lower Woods** is a gate and information board. Ignore this entrance to the woodland – instead follow the gravelled track that runs into the wood to the left of the gateway. In 250 yards, where this track bears left, bear right off the track to join a grassy ride. Follow this ride for 175 yards to a metal footbridge over the **Little Avon River**. Cross the river and, beyond the gate ahead, follow a wide grassy ride known as '**Horton Great Trench**'. In 600 yards, look out for a semi-hidden marker post on the left indicating a footpath on the left – this marker post is easy to miss so watch carefully! Just past this post, follow a path on the left through Burnt Wood. Keep on the path

– it drops down into and up out of a small valley – before reaching a gate on the left in 500 yards on the edge of the wood.

② Just before this gate, turn right and follow a track for 375 yards to its junction with **Horton Great Trench**. Turn right along this track and, in 500 yards, you will reach the point where you left the main ride to head into **Burnt Wood**. Continue ahead at this point, retracing your steps along 300 yards of the ride, to an old gateway and path on the left – there is just a single gatepost – ignoring an earlier pair of paths on the same side of the ride. Follow the path beyond this old gateway for 375 yards down to a footbridge over the **Little Avon River**. Cross the river and follow the ride opposite uphill for 350 yards to **Plumber's Trench**, a wide crosstrack. Turn right and follow this track for 600 yards to a gateway and the car park.

Paddling in the Little Avon River.

Hawkesbury Upton and the Cotswold Edge

Taking in the view.

The Cotswold Escarpment, known colloquially as 'The Edge', is where the high open ground of the Cotswold plateau drops steeply away to the Severn Vale. It is this landscape that is explored on this particular walk, which starts off from the village of Hawkesbury Upton, a name to conjure with. 'Bury' means some sort of camp or settlement, with the suffix 'Upton' suggesting a location on high ground. As for the prefix 'Hawk', the image of birds of prey encircling some sort of hilltop encampment does have a vaguely romantic notion. It certainly is a pretty high and exposed location, lying at some 650 ft above sea level.

The walk heads out across the exposed and open ground to the south of the village – so be sure to choose a clear and fine day for this walk – before following a section of the Cotswold Way along the escarpment itself. Here the views are outstanding, stretching way beyond the Severn Vale and its mighty river towards the Forest of Dean and the distant Welsh Hills. Dogs will thoroughly enjoy the wide open expanses of countryside, as well as the enclosed and traffic-free section of the Cotswold Way. They will also enjoy relaxing in the garden of the Beaufort Arms at journey's end.

Terrain

Well-defined tracks and fieldpaths that cross the gently undulating Cotswold plateau.

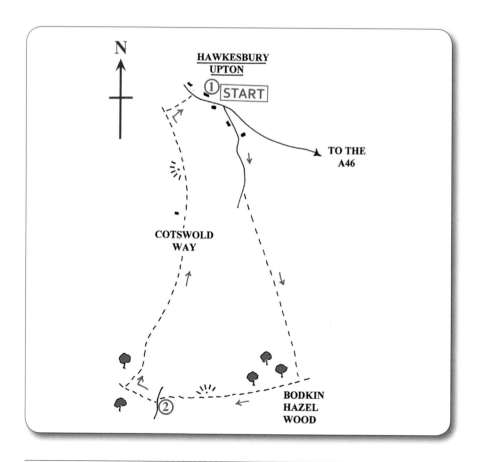

Bristol & Bath – A Dog Walker's Guide

Where to park

The village hall free car park in Hawkesbury Upton (GR ST 778870). **OS map:** Explorer 167 Thornbury, Dursley & Yate.

How to get there

Follow the A46 north from junction 18 of the M4 motorway at Tormarton for 5 miles to Petty France before taking the next left turn, signposted to Hawkesbury Upton. In 1 mile, having passed the Beaufort Arms in Hawkesbury Upton on the left, turn right into the village hall car park.

Nearest refreshments

The Beaufort Arms – a most friendly and welcoming pub – can boast an attractive rear garden where dogs can rest at journey's end. A particular recommendation from the menu would be the faggots, mash and peas, with the faggots being made in the village. ☎ 01454 238217.

Dog factors

Distance: 4 miles.
Road walking: 600 yards of quiet country lane at the start of the walk.
Livestock: With the fields along the way being under crop, livestock are unlikely to be encountered on this walk.
Stiles: None.
Nearest vets: The Rowe Veterinary Hospital, Wotton-under-Edge. ☎ 01453 843295.

The Walk

1 Leave the car park, turn left and walk through **Hawkesbury Upton** for 250 yards before turning right into Sandpits Lane. Follow this lane to the edge of Hawkesbury Upton before continuing for 200 yards to a signposted footpath on the left. Follow this path, it is a wide track, for 400 yards to an open arable field. Keep ahead across this field to pick up the course of a field boundary and follow this boundary – the boundary on the left – down to a gap in the wall in the bottom corner of the field. Continue ahead towards **Bodkin Hazel Wood** then walk up the left edge of this woodland to a gate on the right-hand side. Turn right and follow a grassy path ahead – **Bodkin Hazel Lane** – for

Hawkesbury Pool.

close on 1 mile to a gate and lane. Turn left and, in a few paces, right onto a woodland path.

2 Follow this path downhill through the woodland for 350 yards to a marker post and junction. Turn right onto the **Cotswold Way** and follow this path to a gate on the edge of the woodland. Continue on a path that bears half-left uphill and, where the sunken area of trees and bushes on the left ends, keep ahead across the field to a wooden barrier in its far left corner. Beyond this barrier, follow the right edges of two fields to reach a gateway on the right and a track. Follow this track – it is still the Cotswold Way – to the left for ¾ mile to a point where a footpath crosses the track, ignoring a path crossing the track some 250 yards earlier. Turn right at this point – there is an aerial mast ahead – and follow the left edges of two fields through to the main road in **Hawkesbury Upton**. Turn right back to the car park and the **Beaufort Arms**.

Castle Combe and the By Brook Valley

Castle Combe and the By Brook.

Visitors to Castle Combe must experience a real sense of déjà vu. This is the village that has featured in magazines such as *This England* and *The Countryman* on countless occasions, with its stone cottages, market cross and the centuries-old bridge spanning the By Brook also having graced many a greetings card, jigsaw puzzle and calendar. The walk initially follows

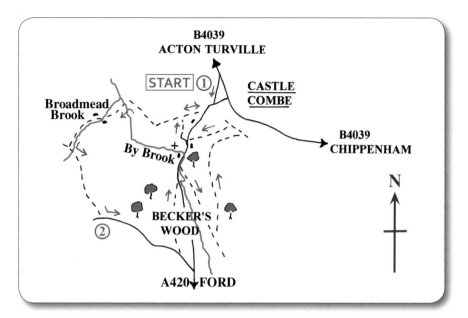

B4039
ACTON TURVILLE

START ①

CASTLE
COMBE

Broadmead
Brook

B4039
CHIPPENHAM

By Brook

N

BECKER'S
WOOD

②

A420 FORD

the Broadmead Brook through a delightful area of woodland, splattered with colour in the spring as bluebells, primroses and violets burst forth. Beyond an ancient clapper bridge, woodland paths pass through Becker's Wood and Parsonage Wood, with a fine beech ride being one particular highlight along the way.

Dogs will love the woodland sections of the walk where they can run free and, with the cooperation of their owners, fetch and carry any number of sticks. And if your dog enjoys water, the Broadmead Brook will prove quite the perfect spot to splash around and cool down on summer days. It is advisable to keep your dog on its lead until you have passed the greens of the local golf course at the outset, as well as during the brief visit to Castle Combe at the end of the walk.

Terrain

Mostly riverside and woodland paths that are well defined and easy to walk. There are a couple of moderate climbs along the way, but nothing too demanding.

Where to park

The Castle Combe visitors' car park (free) alongside the B4039 Acton Turville to Chippenham road (GR ST 845777). **OS map:** Explorer 156 Chippenham & Bradford-on-Avon.

Bristol & Bath – A Dog Walker's Guide

How to get there

From the A420 at Ford between Bristol and Chippenham, follow the unclassified road signposted to Castle Combe. Drive through the village, following the signs for the 'Visitors' Car Park' that lies at the top of the village alongside the B4039.

Nearest refreshments

The walk passes through part of Castle Combe towards journey's end. Here, the White Hart has a delightful courtyard garden, ideal for dogs. Being located in a tourist honeypot, the White Hart is open from 11 am until 11 pm every day, and can boast a good range of traditional pub food based upon locally-sourced ingredients on its menu. ☎ 01249 782295.

The Walk

. . . .

1 Leave the car park and follow the road to the right down to a junction. Turn right and, in 50 yards, veer right into **School Lane**. In 100 yards, on a right-hand bend, pass through a gap in a fence on the left and follow a path that borders a fence on the left. Keep on the path as it runs along the left edge of a golf green before dropping downhill to a stile ahead. Ignoring this stile, follow the path as it bears right and continue for 300 yards until it joins a metalled road in the heart of the golf course. Follow this road to the right for 25 yards before bearing left to cross the **By Brook**. In 200 yards, veer left onto a waymarked path that leaves the golf course and follow the **Broadmead Brook** on the right along to a gate in 200 yards. Cross the river and immediately past the first property on the left ahead, turn left and follow

Dog factors

. . . .

Distance: 4 miles.
Road walking: 200 yards at the beginning and end in Castle Combe; 600 yards of very quiet country lane along the way between the Broadmead Brook and Becker's Wood.
Livestock: None.
Stiles: One that is easy to negotiate towards journey's end.
Nearest vets: Chalkland Vets in Chippenham.
☎ 01249 588805.

Broadmead Brook is perfect for a doggy paddle.

a path that continues to follow the river. In 300 yards, at a junction, turn left and cross the river on a stone bridge. Follow the track ahead uphill for ½ mile to a quiet lane.

② Follow this lane to the left for ½ mile and, shortly past the drive leading to **Shrub Farm**, follow a footpath on the left into **Becker's Wood** to reach the Ford to Castle Combe road in 600 yards. Turn left and, in 100 yards, cross a footbridge on the right over the **By Brook** and follow an enclosed path along to a handgate and field. Follow the right edge of the field uphill for 250 yards and, a few paces before a marker post on the left, turn sharply left and follow a grassy path that continues to climb steeply up the hill to enter woodland. In ½ mile, beyond a wooden barrier, turn left along a track and, in a few paces, turn left onto a footpath. Follow this path down to the road in **Castle Combe**. Turn left to the **Market Cross** before turning right up past the **Castle Inn Hotel** to **Archway Cottage**. Follow the back lane beyond this property to the left – and shortly right – around to **Gardeners House**. Continue uphill on a stony path, passing under a bridge, to reach a stile. Beyond this stile, retrace your steps along the path that borders the golf course before rejoining **School Lane**. Continue ahead, taking the first left back to the car park.

Marshfield

Looking towards Marshfield.

It is difficult to imagine but, in the days before the M4 motorway and various other traffic improvements, Marshfield's High Street formed part of the main road linking Bristol and London. An impressive High Street it is too, running for some half a mile from Nicholas Crispe's almshouses of 1612 at its western end to the great tower of St Mary the Virgin church at the other. This is the setting each Boxing Day for a play performed by the Marshfield Mummers who, dressed in costumes made from strips of paper, perform their play at several locations along the High Street.

Marshfield lies on the undulating Cotswold plateau, with nothing more than a gentle climb here and there along the way. Dogs will love the green lanes, where there is every opportunity to run free without hindrance from

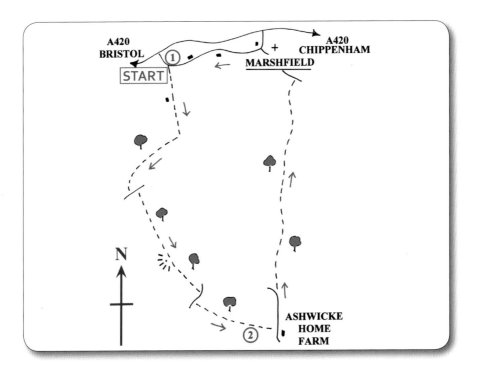

cattle, stiles or traffic. The final mile back into Marshfield also crosses a swathe of open countryside that dogs will thoroughly enjoy. A couple of fields may contain livestock, but these are nosey rather than aggressive creatures.

Dog factors
. . . .
Distance: 4 miles.
Road walking: Pavement walking the length of Marshfield's High Street at journey's end. And 300 yards of Ashwicke Road, a quiet lane between Ashwicke Home Farm and West Lodge.
Livestock: Occasionally in one or two fields on the final mile of fieldpath back into Marshfield.
Stiles: None.
Nearest vets: Chalkland Vets in Chippenham.
☎ 01249 588805.

Terrain

An undulating landscape with one or two gentle climbs along the way.

Where to park

The roadside at the western end of Marshfield's High Street by the almshouses (GR ST 773734). **OS map:** Explorer 155 Bristol & Bath.

How to get there

Approaching from the west, follow the A420 from Cold Ashton, where it crosses the A46 north of Bath, towards Chippenham. In 2 miles, turn right into Marshfield and the almshouses are on the left-hand side as you join the High Street.

Nearest refreshments

Marshfield's High Street boasts the Catherine Wheel, where well-behaved dogs on leads are allowed in the bar. And the Catherine Wheel even says that if a dog water bowl is not available then please ask for one! ☎ 01225 892220.

One of the quiet paths along the way.

*Almshouses on
Marshfield's
High Street.*

The Walk

● ●

❶ With your back to the almshouses, follow the road to the right for 10 yards before turning left by a tollhouse into **Green Lane**. Follow this back lane – beyond the last property on the right it becomes a track – for ¾ mile through to a lane, ignoring stiles and paths on the left and right along the way. Turn left and, in 50 yards, turn right along a bridleway. In ¾ mile, cross a farm access road and continue following the track for 250 yards through to **Ayford Lane**. Turn right and, in 75 yards, left onto an enclosed path. Follow this path for ¼ mile through to an open field before following its right-hand boundary through to a gate and **Ashwicke Road**.

2 Turn left and, on a left-hand bend in 300 yards by **West Lodge**, pass through a handgate and cross the field ahead to a gate in the opposite field boundary. Go over a drive to a gate opposite before crossing the corner of a field to another gate. Walk the length of the next field to another gate, before crossing the next field – keeping to the right of a line of trees – to reach a gate in the bottom corner of the field. Walk down the left edge of the next field to another gate before walking down the right edge of the next field to another gate. Continue ahead in the direction of Marshfield to another gate just beyond a tree. Follow the path beyond this gate up to a lane in **Marshfield**. Follow this lane to the left, keeping left at the next junction, back up to Marshfield's **High Street**. Turn left and walk the length of the High Street back to the almshouses.

Marshfield's fine 15th-century church.

Lansdown and North Stoke

North Stoke, seen from across the fields.

Lansdown Hill, high above Bath, was the site of a bloody battle in the Civil War. Despite losing as many as 300 men, and with many more wounded, the Royalists won the day, with one observer noting that 'legs and arms were flying all over the place'. This is certainly a lofty hilltop perch with views at every turn, quite the place to defend against attack. Early on, the view extends to the west across the Severn Vale and Bristol towards the distant Welsh Hills. And then we find ourselves on the fringes of Bath Racecourse at the wonderfully named 'Prospect Stile', which is now in fact a gate. From here the outlook is to the south, across the Avon Valley towards the Mendip Hills.

North Stoke, the one village along the way, is a pretty enough place. There is St Martin's church, to quote, 'perched on a throne that nature gave it', as well as the double-gabled Manor House Farm and the 17th-century Manor Farm with a distinctive shell hood over its porch. At the top of the village, opposite the church, there is a medieval pavement. It was constructed not only to keep the feet dry but also to help in the loading of carts. Above the village is Little Down hillfort. Being on a dry hilltop well away from water supplies, this was in all probability a temporary defensive site to which locals would flock in the event of an attack.

The great appeal of this walk is the almost total absence of road walking. Field paths, tracks and open hillsides provide the perfect location for dogs to simply run free without the constraints of a leash or the fear of traffic.

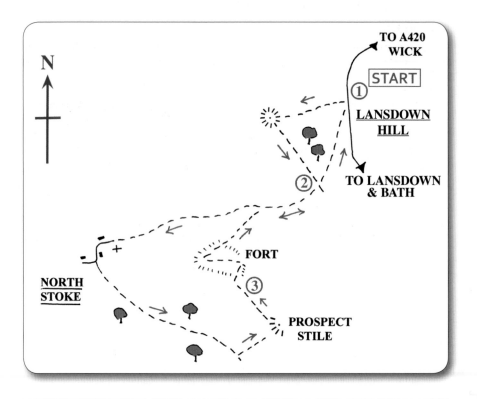

Dog factors
· ·

Distance: 5 miles.
Road walking: A short section of quiet road walking in North Stoke, and 200 yards on the main road across Lansdown at the end of the walk where dogs will need to be kept under control.
Livestock: Sheep occasionally graze on the land above North Stoke village.
Stiles: None.
Nearest vets: Bath Veterinary Centre. ☎ 01225 313995.

Terrain
Level hilltops, with one climb up to Prospect Stile.

Where to park
Roadside on Lansdown Hill in the vicinity of the Bevil Grenville Monument (GR ST 721702). **OS map:** Explorer 155 Bristol & Bath.

How to get there
Drive up onto Lansdown Hill from Bath and, ½ mile on from the entrance to Bath Racecourse, park on the right in a rough parking area that gives access to the Bevil Grenville Civil War Monument. This is opposite a left turn that leads to the Avon Fire & Rescue Service Fire Control Centre. If coming from Bristol, leave the A420 at Wick and follow the road uphill onto Lansdown. The parking area is then on the left, ½ mile before Bath Racecourse.

Nearest refreshments
Drive back towards Bath from the parking area and, in ¾ mile, the Blathwayt Arms lies alongside the road. With excellent food, and fine real ales from Bath Ales, this is just the place to rest and linger awhile at journey's end. There is an extensive garden that is just perfect for dogs, too. ☎ 01225 421995.

The Walk
· ·

❶ Cross the road and follow the access road down to the entrance to the **Avon Fire & Rescue Service Fire Control Centre**. At this point, follow a road on the right for 50 yards to a footpath on the left, waymarked as the **Cotswold**

The monument that marks the site of the Civil War battle of 1643.

Way. Follow this path along to a gate before continuing along the top left edge of a hillside field to a Civil War information board and handgate in the corner of the field. Turn left through this handgate and follow the right edge of the field ahead across to a handgate by some conifers. Pass through a small enclosure, a golf green to the left, to reach a handgate and track. Follow this track to the left – it borders a golf course – to reach a junction of paths in ½ mile where the woodland on the left ends.

2 Turn right along a path signposted as 'Cotswold Way Bridlepath' and continue across the golf course for 600 yards to reach a handgate. Follow the bridleway ahead downhill for 600 yards to a gate and continue ahead to the road in **North Stoke** just below the church. Follow this road ahead for 200 yards to a point where it bears left and then right. On the right-hand bend, keep ahead along a side road that passes a number of properties. Where the metalled road ends, follow a track across the hillside for close on 1 mile to a junction of paths. Pass through a gate on the left and follow a path ahead up the right edge of **Shiner's Wood** to reach a gate. Continue following a path to the left to reach a gate and topograph at the point shown on the OS map as **Prospect Stile**. Turn left and follow a path across the edge of **Bath Race Course**.

3 Beyond a gate at the end of the race course, walk along the left edge of the next field before bearing right along the end field boundary. In 150 yards, at a marker post, turn left and walk across the middle of **Little Down Hill Fort**. On the far side of the enclosure, pass through a gateway and drop downhill to a marker post. Turn right and walk across a field to a gate before following a grassy path down to the track followed earlier in the walk. Turn right and continue to a gate before retracing your steps ahead across the golf course to reach a junction of paths in 600 yards. Continue ahead on a path that borders woodland on the left to reach a gate in 600 yards. Beyond this gate, follow a lane up to the main road running across **Lansdown Hill**. Turn left and follow a verge back to the parking area.

It's only a shower!

Hanham Mills and the River Avon

Hanham Gorge.

Although less well known than the Avon Gorge in Bristol, Hanham Gorge between Bristol and Bath is certainly one of the more attractive stretches of the River Avon. It was not always peace and tranquillity along this stretch of water, however. An Act of Parliament passed in 1712 gave the power to construct the Avon Navigation. By 1727, six locks and other related works had made the river navigable through to Bath. The local coal miners were displeased at the large volume of Shropshire coal that began to appear in the area courtesy of the new navigation. Having travelled to the West Country by way of the River Severn, it was seen as a clear threat to their livelihood. The miners' reactions were sometimes violent, and included

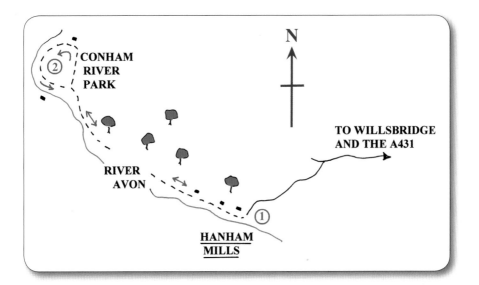

on one occasion the destruction of the lock at nearby Saltford. None of the culprits were apprehended, which was probably as well with 'damaging the navigation' being an offence that carried the death penalty.

Today, the riverside walk from Hanham Mills through to Conham River Park is an absolute delight. Swans and ducks, coots and herons are all a common sight along the river, whilst the sharp-eyed visitor might even catch a glimpse of a kingfisher, whose blue and orange features are unmistakable. Dogs will love the sounds and smells of the woodland that borders the river, as well as the chance to swim in the river at various points along the way. With a total absence of stiles, livestock and traffic, this is quite the perfect walk for a dog.

Terrain

Flat riverside paths throughout. An easy and straightforward there-and-back walk.

Where to park

The free public car park alongside the Chequers Inn at Hanham Mills (GR ST 648700). **OS map:** Explorer 155 Bristol & Bath.

How to get there

Leave the A431 Bristol to Bath road ¾ mile west of Bitton Station on the Avon Valley Railway, and follow Court Farm Road for 600 yards to the entrance to Hanham Court. At this point, turn left onto an easily missed cul de sac and

Bristol & Bath – A Dog Walker's Guide

Dog factors

Distance: 4½ miles.
Road walking: None.
Livestock: None.
Stiles: None.
Nearest vets: Fernlea Veterinary Clinic in Hanham.
☎ 0117 967 7067.

follow what is a narrow lane down to the car park at Hanham Mills by the River Avon.

Nearest refreshments

A unique feature at Conham is Beeses Bar and Tea Gardens, described as 'beguiling and bewitching' by one commentator. Opened in 1846 by a Mrs Beese, what makes the tea gardens unique is access by means of the oldest river ferry crossing the Avon. The tea gardens are open in the afternoon on Friday, Saturday and Sunday. Check the website www.beeses.co.uk for more information on opening times. The riverside gardens of both the Chequers Inn (☎ 0117 329 1711) and the Old Lock and Weir (☎ 0117 960 9345) at Hanham Mills are also perfect places for dogs and their owners to rest at journey's end.

The Walk

1 From the car park, walk down to the **River Avon** and turn right by the Chequers Inn along a road giving access to a number of properties. In 200 yards, at a fork, keep left along a path signposted as the '**Avon River Path**'. Having passed underneath the **Avon Ring Road**, continue following the riverside path for 1¾ miles to a junction by a shelter opposite **Beeses Tea Gardens**. Turn right, following the side path uphill.

2 In 150 yards, just before this path reaches a gate and a road, turn left through a gap in a wall and follow the path ahead to a junction. Turn right down to a gate and the **Conham River Park car park**. Leave this car park via a gate on the left on a path waymarked '**The River Avon Trail**'. Walk down to the river, turn left and follow the Avon upstream back to the shelter and junction passed earlier. Retrace your steps along the riverbank back to **Hanham Mills**.

The attractive woodland that borders the Avon.

Snuff Mills and the River Frome

The footbridge near the start of the walk.

At **Snuff Mills,** just a couple of miles from Bristol's city centre, the River Frome runs through a valley with steep wooded sides and some exposed rock faces. Purchased by Bristol City Council in 1926, the site

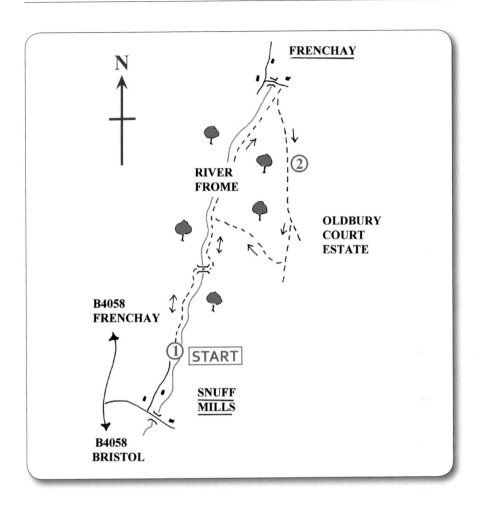

N

FRENCHAY

RIVER
FROME

②

OLDBURY
COURT
ESTATE

B4058
FRENCHAY

① START

SNUFF
MILLS

B4058
BRISTOL

was viewed as 'a pleasure walk for citizens of Bristol'. There were a number of mills along this stretch of the Frome, with local legend maintaining that the area's name originated from one of the millers. His nickname was 'Snuffy Jack' because his smock was always covered in snuff.

Dogs will love this walk ... and not only because of the absence of traffic, stiles and livestock. If your dog enjoys swimming, there are numerous safe access points to the River Frome. And being surrounded by woodland, there is every opportunity to retrieve sticks from the river. This is also immensely popular dog-walking country, with lots of other canine friends to be found along the way.

Bristol & Bath – A Dog Walker's Guide

Terrain

With just the occasional gentle climb along the way, this is a very straightforward walk. A short section of the riverside path can be muddy underfoot following heavy rainfall.

Where to park

The free public car park at the entrance to the Snuff Mills Park (GR ST 623766). **OS map:** Explorer 155 Bristol & Bath.

How to get there

The B4058 runs from Frenchay through Stapleton to the centre of Bristol. At a mini-roundabout 1 mile south of Frenchay Hospital, turn southwards into Broomhill Road. In 200 yards, turn left into River View and drive along to the car park at the entrance to Snuff Mills Park.

Nearest refreshments

In the car park there is a refreshment hut that sells drinks, confectionary and light snacks.

Dog factors

Distance: 2½ miles.
Road walking: None.
Livestock: None.
Stiles: None.
Nearest vets: The Zetland Veterinary Group in Fishponds.
☎ 0117 965 4413.

The Walk

1 Walk to the far end of the car park and follow a path alongside the **Frome** for ¼ mile to a bridge. Cross the river, turn left and continue following the river for ¾ mile until it reaches a flight of steps and a path leading to the road by a bridge in **Frenchay**. Turn right along this path and follow it uphill for 200 yards until it emerges onto the open ground of **Oldbury Court Park**.

2 Follow the tarmac path ahead for 300 yards until it drops down into woodland to cross a stream. Beyond this stream, continue following the tarmac path

The popular riverside path.

to a fork on another area of open ground. Keep right and, as the path approaches a play area, turn right onto a path that drops downhill back to the **River Frome**. Turn left and follow the riverside path for 350 yards back to the footbridge crossed earlier in the walk. Cross the river once again and follow the path to the left back to the car park.

Can I go for a paddle?

The Blaise Castle Estate

The 18th-century sham castle above the gorge.

The Blaise Castle Estate is a gem of a location that can boast wooded limestone cliffs, a folly castle, a grand mansion that houses a collection of artefacts depicting social history and an ancient hill fort high on Kings Weston Hill. The whole is set in grounds originally designed by Humphry Repton. Human activity on the site dates back over 2,000 years and, following its ownership by a succession of wealthy owners who viewed it very much as a 'pleasure park', it was finally purchased by the Corporation of Bristol in 1926 for the princely sum of just £20,175.

The various points of interest include the Beech Cathedral – a stand of beech planted in the 18th century, the Lily Pond that dates from the mid

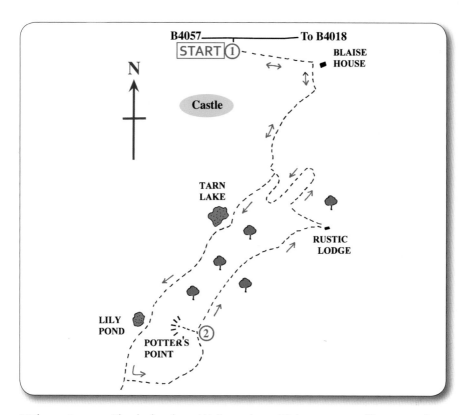

19th century, a Rhododendron Walk and an 18th-century mill removed to its current site from West Harptree in 1952 when nearby countryside was flooded to create the Chew Valley Reservoir. A dramatic highlight is Potter's Point, a steep-sided viewpoint across the wooded gorge.

This is a totally traffic-free route where dogs will enjoy the freedom to roam and meet other canines, though they should be kept close near Potter's Point. The woodland sections also provide plenty of sticks that dogs can chase and retrieve.

Terrain

The walk follows well-defined paths and tracks in the Blaise Castle Estate, with some not insignificant climbs along the way.

Where to park

The public car park (free) at the Blaise Castle Estate (GR ST 559786). **OS map:** Explorer 155 Bristol & Bath.

Dog factors

Distance: 3 miles.
Road walking: None.
Livestock: None.
Stiles: None.
Nearest vets: Viking Vets in nearby Henbury. ☎ 0117 950 5888.

How to get there

Leave the M5 motorway at junction 17 and follow the A4018, signposted to West Bristol. In 1½ miles, at the third roundabout on from the M5, turn right onto the B4057. In ¾ mile, with Henbury church on the left, keep ahead on a one-way system. The car park for Blaise Castle is on the left in 250 yards.

Nearest refreshments

The Blaise Castle Café is open at normal business hours every day and is just a short walk from the car park. It sells a wide range of snacks and meals, as well as hot and cold drinks. ☎ Blaise Castle on 0117 903 9818 for information.

The Walk

❶ From the car park, walk along to the **Blaise Castle Café** and continue along the path towards **Blaise House**. At a junction just before the house, turn right and follow a path that drops downhill into a wooded gorge. On reaching the valley bottom, cross **Mill Bridge** and follow the path to the right, **Hazel Brook** on the right. Continue for 200 yards to reach **Tarn Lake** before keeping on the tarmac path through the valley bottom for 300 yards to reach **Lily Pond**. Cross the brook and, towards the top of a gentle climb, turn left off the main path to descend some steps to reach Hazel Brook. Turn to the left across a sluice before turning right to follow the course of the brook. Shortly, turn left onto a flight of steps bordered by a wall.

❷ Partway up what is a steep climb, turn left at a marker through a gap in a wall to follow a path uphill to visit the spectacular lookout point known as **Potter's Point**. Retrace your steps to the marker post and continue following the path uphill. At the top of the climb, follow a path to the left that runs alongside

The atmospheric Beech Cathedral.

Henbury Golf Course. Continue following the path across the hilltop, keeping left at all forks, to reach what is known as '**Main Drive**' by the '**Rustic Lodge**'. Turn left and follow this surfaced path down past **Woodman's Cottage**, and back into the valley bottom. Cross **Mill Bridge** and retrace your steps to the right back to the café and car park, detouring into the woodland along the way should you wish to find **Blaise Castle** itself.

Leigh Woods and the Avon Gorge

Impressive limestone cliffs line the gorge.

This outstanding walk starts off in Leigh Woods, where a path drops gently downhill through deciduous woodland to reach the banks of the River Avon deep in the Avon Gorge. All around are towering limestone cliffs with the Clifton Suspension Bridge high overhead. Designed by Brunel, it was opened in 1861 at a cost of some £100,000. It stands 245 ft above the river and has a span of 702 ft. Suicides were historically common from the

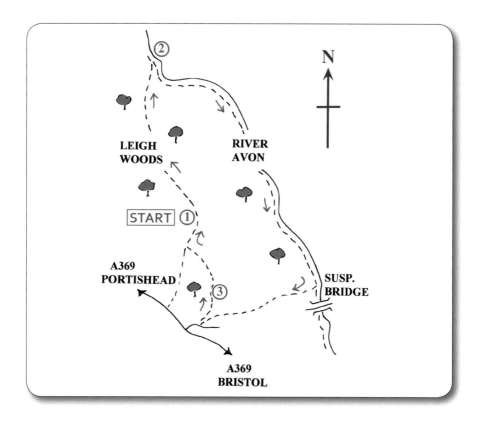

bridge, the biggest failure being a Victorian lady whose attempt was foiled when her billowing skirts acted as a parachute. She descended slowly and safely to land in the soft mud below – the tide was out!

Beyond the gorge, the walk climbs up from the river through Nightingale Valley. This is one of the most important woodland sites on lowland carboniferous limestone in the country, and contains two unique species – the Bristol whitebeam and the Bristol rock cress. Easier to find, and perhaps of more general interest, are the rich collection of fungi in the reserve. During the autumn months, many colourful specimens appear, such as the poisonous red and the white fly agaric.

Dogs will love the woodland sections of the walk, with sticks and smells and sounds aplenty. It might be sensible to keep the water-loving ones under control on the riverside section of the walk, with the Avon hereabouts being tidal and strong.

Bristol & Bath – A Dog Walker's Guide

Dog factors
....

Distance: 3½ miles.
Road walking: None.
Livestock: None.
Stiles: None.
Nearest vets: The Highcroft Veterinary Group has a branch at nearby Ashton. ☎ 0117 953 0707.

Terrain

Well-defined paths; a gentle descent through Leigh Woods followed by a steep ascent through Nightingale Valley.

Where to park

The free public car park at Leigh Woods (GR ST 553740). **OS map:** Explorer 155 Bristol & Bath.

How to get there

Approaching from the Bristol direction, take the A369 Bristol to Portishead road to its junction with the B3129, which is 2 miles west of Ashton Gate; 250 yards beyond the traffic lights at this junction, turn right onto a driveway leading into the Forestry Commission's Leigh Woods. Follow this driveway for 800 yards to a car park.

Nearest refreshments

Drive west along the A369 for ½ mile to Abbots Leigh to find the George Inn. The large garden and patio area will prove welcoming for dogs whilst their owners enjoy a dish from the imaginative menu. ☎ 01275 376985.

The Walk
....

1 Walk down to the bottom end of the car park and follow a forestry road to the left signposted 'Paradise Bottom – On Foot Only'. In 150 yards, ignore a track going off on the right, keeping ahead on the main track instead for another 150 yards to **Oakwood Lodge**. Keep on the track ahead beyond Oakwood Lodge for ¼ mile, ignoring all side turns, to a distinct junction – the track ahead continues to **Paradise Bottom** whilst a right turn is waymarked

A shady path through the woodland.

as 'National Cycle Network Route 41'. Turn right and follow a woodland path downhill for 350 yards to a gap in a stone wall and a path alongside the **River Avon**.

2 Turn right and follow the river upstream for 1¾ miles to a point 150 yards before the **Clifton Suspension Bridge**. At this point, turn right under a railway bridge to a gate at the entrance to the National Trust's **Leigh Woods** property. Follow a path uphill for ½ mile before turning left through a gateway to join a road. Turn right for a few paces before turning right through a gap in a wooden barrier to follow a path back into the woodland.

3 On reaching a forestry road, turn right down towards a shed. Just before this shed, turn left along a side track – following blue waymarks – to reach what is called the '**Parish Wall**'. In 50 yards, turn left through a gap in this wall and follow a woodland path back to the driveway leading to the car park. Turn right and, in 250 yards, you will return to the car park.

Ashton Court

In the parkland.

Ashton Court, with its massive 300 ft frontage, is an intriguing blend of styles ranging from Gothic and Jacobean to Tudor. There are even unsubstantiated suggestions that the south-west wing may have been the work of Inigo Jones. This was home for the Smyth family for over 400 years, with Thomas Smyth, an MP in Stuart times, being one of the last landowners to employ a jester. The family fortunes diminished during the 20th century and, in 1959, the whole estate was purchased by Bristol City Council for use as a public amenity. The surrounding grounds, which feature on this walk, were landscaped by Humphry Repton (1752–1818). The delightful parkland extends to some 840 acres, included in which is a noted deer park.

Dogs will enjoy running free across the vast open spaces of the park, with the sight and sound of other dogs never that far away. There is also a lengthy section of walking through ancient deciduous woodland, with many smells and sounds that will certainly excite any dog's senses.

Terrain

An undulating landscape with one or two gentle climbs along the way.

Where to park

The public car park by Ashton Court (GR ST 558719). **OS map:** Explorer 155 Bristol & Bath.

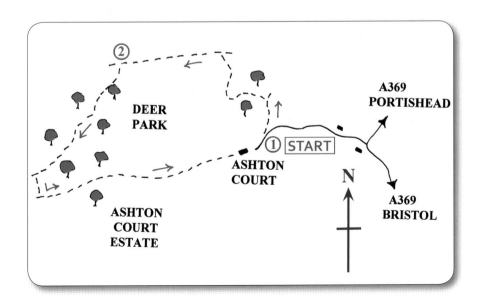

Bristol & Bath – A Dog Walker's Guide

Dog factors
. . . .
Distance: 2½ miles.
Road walking: None.
Livestock: None.
Stiles: None.
Nearest vets: The Highcroft Veterinary Group has a branch at nearby Ashton. ☎ 0117 953 0707.

How to get there
Leave the A369 Bristol to Portishead road at Bower Ashton and follow Kennel Lodge Road past the University of the West of England's Art College and through to the Ashton Court car park. The estate opens at 8 am each day and closes around dusk. Please visit their website for exact seasonal closing times: www.ashtoncourtestate.co.uk

Nearest refreshments
The Courtyard Café at Ashton Court offers tea, coffee and a wide variety of hot and cold food and drink. Seating and tables are available both inside the café and outside beneath a glass canopy in the old stables courtyard – a great place for dogs to relax. ☎ 0117 963 9176.

The Walk
. . . .

1 Walk to the opposite end of the car park from **Ashton Court** and, where the road bears right, pass through a gap in the fence ahead and follow a gravelled path that bears left over to a gate at the entrance to **Ashton Court Deer Park**. Do not pass through this gate – instead turn left up towards some woodland. As the path enters the woodland, turn right and follow a path that winds its way uphill through the trees to reach a fence at the far end of the woodland. Turn left and follow the line of the fence as far as a gate on the right. Pass through this gateway, turn right and follow the fence bordering the deer park for 150 yards to a gate and a path coming out of the park. Turn left and follow a gravelled path for 50 yards to an estate road. Cross this road and continue following the gravel path ahead uphill for 350 yards to a fork.

2 Bear left down to an area of woodland, follow the main path ahead down to a T-junction and turn right. Follow this woodland path for ½ mile to a point

The west entrance of Ashton Court.

where it bears sharply to the right and a side track drops downhill. Turn left down this side path and drop downhill to a T-junction. Turn left and follow a path that emerges from the woodland in 600 yards, with the deer park on the left. Continue ahead along the main track for 350 yards to a junction and follow the estate road to the right. In 250 yards, walk across an area of grassland to reach **Ashton Court**. Pass through a gate on the right and follow a path along the imposing east-facing frontage of the mansion. At the far end of this path, pass through a gate back into the car park.

Clevedon and the Bristol Channel

On the coastal path.

The sea, with its ebb and flow of tides, has long held a fascination and delight for everyone from the youngest toddler to the aged octogenarian. Clevedon, an archetypal English seaside resort, lies on

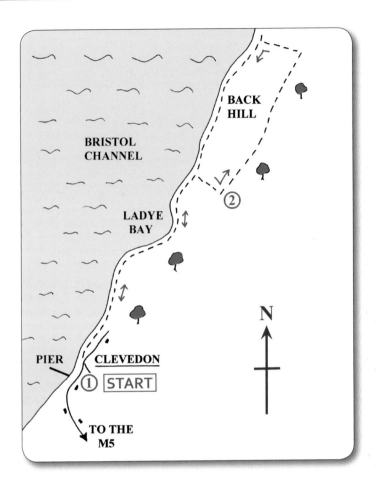

the Bristol Channel coast a few miles to the south-west of Bristol. The town sits somewhat sedately overlooking the channel, on a rocky and pebbly stretch of the coastline. The atmosphere is very Victorian, with large and grey limestone villas, public parks and bowling greens, although Georgian and Regency buildings speak of the town's gradual development from a fishing village to a small, fashionable resort during the 19th century. The jewel in the crown is the town's pier, of which John Betjeman wrote that it 'recalls a painting by Turner, or an etching by Whistler or Sickert, or even a Japanese print ... Without its Pier, Clevedon would be a diamond with a flaw.' This was written at a time when a section of the pier had collapsed and the future of this iconic structure was under threat.

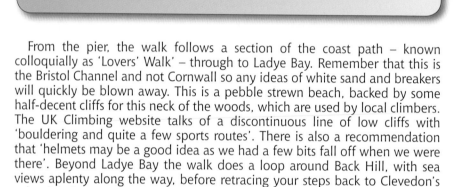

Dog factors

Distance: 4½ miles.
Road walking: 200 yards of road walking with a pavement at the start/finish of the walk between Clevedon Pier and Lovers' Walk.
Livestock: None.
Stiles: None.
Nearest vets: Alexandra Vets in Clevedon. ☎ 01275 343457.

From the pier, the walk follows a section of the coast path – known colloquially as 'Lovers' Walk' – through to Ladye Bay. Remember that this is the Bristol Channel and not Cornwall so any ideas of white sand and breakers will quickly be blown away. This is a pebble strewn beach, backed by some half-decent cliffs for this neck of the woods, which are used by local climbers. The UK Climbing website talks of a discontinuous line of low cliffs with 'bouldering and quite a few sports routes'. There is also a recommendation that 'helmets may be a good idea as we had a few bits fall off when we were there'. Beyond Ladye Bay the walk does a loop around Back Hill, with sea views aplenty along the way, before retracing your steps back to Clevedon's splendid pier.

Dogs will love the shingle beaches at both Clevedon and Ladye Bay. With driftwood to fetch and retrieve, and gentle waves splashing along the foreshore, these are quite perfect spots for water-loving dogs.

Terrain

Level coast path, with a stiff but short climb onto Back Hill. This climb can be avoided by doing a there-and-back walk along the coast path.

Where to park

On the seafront below the pier (GR ST 402719). **OS map:** Explorer 154 Bristol West & Portishead.

How to get there

Leave the M5 at junction 20 and follow the signs to Clevedon's seafront. Park in the vicinity of the pier, where the walk starts.

Nearest refreshments

There is a selection of pubs and cafés along Clevedon's seafront but, with dogs allowed on the beach, why not pack a picnic to enjoy by the sea?

Looking out over the Channel.

The Walk

. . . .

1 With your back to the pier entrance, follow the road – **Marine Parade** – uphill to the left for 200 yards to its junction with **Marine Hill** by the local Catholic church. Walk ahead for a few paces before veering left onto a tarmac path known locally as '**Lovers' Walk**'. Follow this coastal path for ½ mile to a junction above **Ladye Bay**. Ignoring the stepped path on the left that drops down to the bay, keep ahead on the main coastal path for 350 yards to a right turn at a point where a piece of wooden boarding covers the path. Turn right at this point, heading uphill from the coast, to reach the hilltop in 300 yards.

Strolling along Clevedon's pier.

2 Turn left and follow a path across the hilltop to reach a gate and stile in 300 yards and a junction. Walk ahead a few paces, pass through a gateway and continue following the enclosed path across the hilltop. In ¾ mile, at a junction, pass through the gateway on the left and walk down the right edge of the field ahead to a stile in its bottom corner and the coastal path. Follow the path for 1¾ miles back to its junction with **Marine Hill** by the Catholic church. Turn right down **Marine Parade** to return to the pier.

Bourton Combe

Along the way.

A **'combe' is normally defined as** a 'valley or hollow on the side of a hill'. In many cases this would be a wooded valley, making for perfect walking for dogs, with an abundance of sticks to fetch and carry along the way. South-west of Bristol along the main Weston-super-Mare road are a succession of secretive and shady combes – Cheston Combe and Tap's Combe, Brockley Combe and Cleve Combe, as well as dog-walking country par excellence in the shape of Bourton Combe. Centred upon a delightful limestone gorge, the surrounding woodland is dominated by indigenous yew and elder trees, many of which grow out of crannies in the rock faces. With a complete absence of stiles, cattle and roads, this is the perfect dog walk.

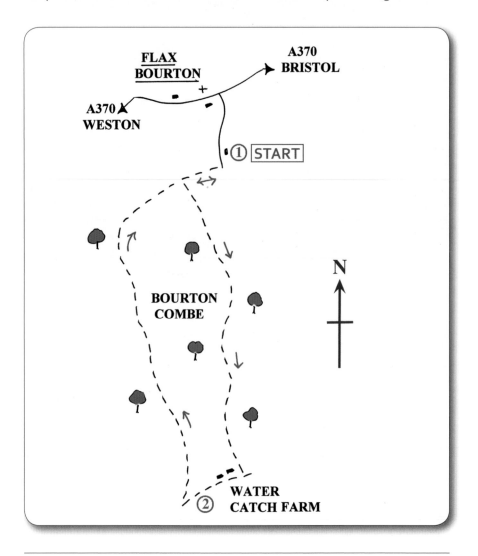

Dog factors
· ·
Distance: 2½ miles.
Road walking: None.
Livestock: None.
Stiles: None.
Nearest vets: Susan Yeo in nearby Backwell. ☎ 01275 462691.

Terrain
The walk follows well-defined paths and tracks in and around Bourton Combe. Some of the paths are stony underfoot and, being shady woodland, there can be the occasional muddy patch.

Where to park
Roadside parking for a few vehicles at the end of a cul de sac lane giving access to Bourton Combe (GR ST 508690). **OS map:** Explorer 154 Bristol West & Portishead.

How to get there
Driving through Flax Bourton from the Bristol direction on the A370, turn left into a turning signposted 'Bourton Combe' just before passing the church on the right. Park on the roadside at the end of this cul de sac lane in 350 yards.

Nearest refreshments
The Jubilee Inn in the centre of Flax Bourton offers a wide selection of food choices. Dogs are welcome in the bar area and in the garden, which is a delightful spot on a sunny day. ☎ 01275 462797.

The Walk
· ·

1 At the end of the lane, follow the track on the right, signposted to **Barrow Common**. In 250 yards, by a section of wall, turn left at a junction to follow a path along the eastern edge of the woodland. Follow this woodland path for just over ¾ mile to a gateway immediately before **Water Catch Farm**. Follow the path ahead to the left of the farm buildings, before turning right to follow a path along past a cottage and back into the woodland.

Finn, ready for the off!

2 In 300 yards, with a ruinous building on the left and a quarry warning sign on the right, turn right at a junction and follow a woodland path for 600 yards to a fork. Take the left-hand path and, in 600 yards, at the next junction, take the right-hand path that climbs uphill out of **Bourton Combe**. In 150 yards, on reaching the junction passed at the outset by the stone wall, retrace your steps ahead back to the lane and roadside parking.

Mendip Highpoints

Dolebury Warren.

his is the longest and most challenging walk in the book, climbing
as it does to Blackdown, at 1,067 ft above sea level the literal highpoint
on all Mendip. Fit and active dogs who enjoy wide open spaces will
simply love this walk, with vast areas in which to run free, as well as small
sections of woodland and the occasional valley with its water course.

The Mendip Hills stretch from Frome to Weston-super-Mare. This limestone
mass is best-known for its extensive network of cliffs and underground
caverns, which have been carved out of the limestone by the action of water
over many thousands of years. It is a bleak and lonely landscape, criss-crossed
by ancient tracks and with numerous mounds that testify to the historical

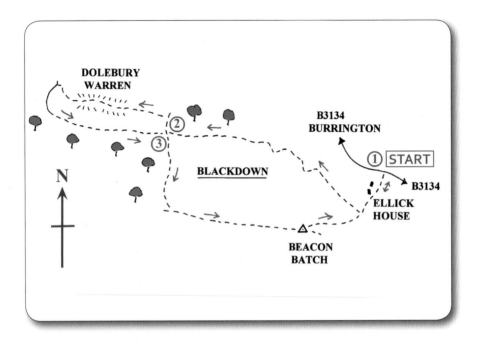

importance of the region. The views from the hillfort on Dolebury Warren and from Blackdown are especially fine, taking in the Severn Estuary and the Bristol Channel, the South Wales coast and the more distant Black Mountains. Definitely a walk for a clear and fine day.

Terrain
Some quite significant climbing on the highest ground in the region.

Where to park
The free car park at the top end of Burrington Combe just below Ellick House (GR ST 489581). **OS map:** Explorer 141 Cheddar Gorge & Mendip Hills West.

How to get there
Burrington lies just off of the A368 and 2 miles east of its junction with the A38 at Churchill. Follow the B3134 road from the A368 up through Burrington Combe for 1½ miles to the car park.

Nearest refreshments
The Plume of Feathers, a mile to the east of Burrington Combe in the small village of Rickford, allow dogs in the bar area as long as they are kept on

Dog factors

Distance: 7 miles or 4 miles.
Road walking: 150 yards on the grass verge of the B3134 has to be followed at the start of the walk to reach Ellick House and the Mendip Hills. This section of road walking is repeated at the end.
Livestock: Sheep occasionally graze on the land around Dolebury Warren.
Stiles: None.
Nearest vets: Alexandra Vets in Clevedon. ☎ 01275 343457.

a lead. They pride themselves on their fresh produce so the menu changes regularly. Lunch and dinner are served daily. ☎ 01761 462682.

The Walk

1 Leave the parking area and follow the B3134 to the left for 150 yards before turning right onto a bridleway by **Ellick House**. Follow this track for 200 yards to a gate, walk ahead for 25 yards to a marker post and turn right to follow a path along the bottom edge of the open ground of **Blackdown**. In ½ mile, keep on the path as it drops down into, and up out of, a sheltered valley containing **East Twin Brook**. In 400 yards, keep on the path as it drops downhill into, and uphill out of, a valley containing **West Twin Brook**. Ignoring a right turn just beyond this valley, continue ahead for 400 yards to a crossroads. Keep ahead, following the main path – it shortly veers left – to reach some tree cover. Follow the path alongside these trees, a fence on the right, along to a gate bearing a **Limestone Link** sign. At the next junction, ignore a path on the left, keeping ahead for a few paces to a fork (*).

2 Fork right and, in 50 yards, turn left through a gateway onto the open ground of **Dolebury Warren**. Walk directly ahead across an open field to a gate and stile in the end field boundary. Walk across the next field towards an area of coniferous woodland. On reaching a marker post, bear right along the end of the conifer plantation to reach the next marker post. Bear left and follow a path

(*) For a shorter walk, turn left to the metal barrier noted at the start of point **3**

Finn enjoying the view on Blackdown.

through some tree cover and out onto an open hilltop. Keep ahead across this hilltop to a gate and stile before continuing to the ramparts of **Dolebury Fort**. Drop gently downhill for ¼ mile to reach a path that enters some woodland in **Dolebury Bottom**. Follow this path for 200 yards to a gateway and keep ahead to reach an unmetalled access lane by a property. Follow this lane to the left down past a number of properties to a junction in 150 yards. Turn left and follow a back lane for 200 yards until it reaches a gate. Continue ahead along an unmetalled track for just over 1 mile, the steep hillside of Dolebury Warren on the left, to return to a junction passed earlier in the walk.

❸ Walk ahead for a few paces before turning right. In 50 yards, at a metal barrier, follow a bridleway uphill onto **Blackdown**, passing a coniferous plantation on the right. In 350 yards, cross a wide track and continue uphill for ½ mile to a crossroads on the hilltop. Turn left and walk along to a gateway before following a grassy ride ahead across the open ground of Blackdown. Keep following the path ahead for 1 mile to the trig point on **Beacon Batch**, the trig point being a landmark on the horizon after ½ mile. On reaching the trig point, take the path on the left that goes off at an angle of 90 degrees, ignoring a much sharper left-hand turn. Follow this path downhill for 600 yards to a gate, before following a track down to the B3134. Turn left back to the parking area.

Springtime on Blackdown.

Charterhouse and Velvet Bottom

In Black Rock Reserve.

The walk explores some of the most interesting landscape to be found on Mendip, in and around the isolated hamlet of Charterhouse. The local lead deposits brought the Romans to the area with the lead being used throughout the Empire ... one notable use being to line the Roman baths at nearby Bath. Today, there are spoil tips, horizontal flues and washing pools, all quietly reverting to a more natural landscape.

In the valleys below Charterhouse lie Long Wood, Black Rock and Velvet Bottom – whose very names conjure up a vivid imagery. These locations could not provide a greater contrast, with Long Wood being an area of broadleaved woodland; Black Rock, a mix of grassland, woodland, rock faces and scree; and Velvet Bottom, a dry river valley that has been the scene of extensive lead workings over many centuries.

Dogs will love the freedom to be found in these open spaces, with not a car or stile in sight. The sounds and smells in Long Wood will also intrigue, as will the opportunity to splash around in some nameless stream that disappears into a pot hole in the woodland, only to re-emerge down in Cheddar Gorge several miles away.

Terrain

An undulating landscape with clear paths and no real climbing.

Where to park

The free car park at the Blackmoor lead workings in Charterhouse (GR ST 505557). **OS map:** Explorer 144 Cheddar Gorge & Mendip Hills West.

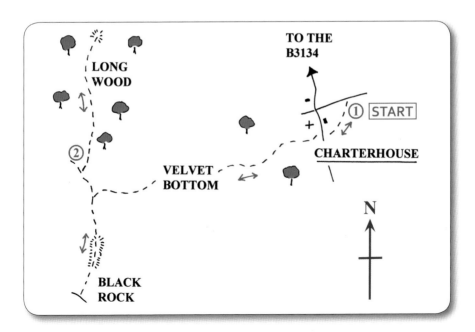

Bristol & Bath – A Dog Walker's Guide

How to get there

Take the B3134, which runs between the A368 and the B3135, and turn off 2 miles south-east of Burrington Combe to follow an unclassified road signposted to Charterhouse. At a minor crossroads in the village, turn left – no signpost – and follow a narrow lane down to the car park.

Nearest refreshments

There are no refreshment facilities within striking distance of this walk. The site of the Blackmoor lead workings at the end of the walk does provide many fine picnicking spots, however. In Cheddar, 4 miles away, there are many cafés, pubs and tea rooms should you wish to eat out.

Dog factors

Distance: 4½ miles.
Road walking: None.
Livestock: None.
Stiles: None.
Nearest vets: Axe Valley Veterinary Practice in Cheddar.
☎ 01934 741292.

The Walk

1 Follow the road out of the parking area and, in 40 yards, pass through a gateway on the left and follow a footpath across 'gruffy ground' (i.e. uneven ground that was formerly small spoil heaps) to a handgate and road. Turn right and, in 25 yards, left along to a gate and **Velvet Bottom**. Follow the path ahead down through Velvet Bottom for 1 mile to a gate and the **Black Rock Reserve**. Turn right and, beyond a gate in 200 yards, veer right to a gate at the entrance to **Long Wood**. Follow the path through Long Wood and, in ½ mile, reach a bridge over a stream. Turn around and retrace your steps through Long Wood to the exit gate.

2 Walk ahead to the gate at the entrance to **Black Rock** and follow the path ahead for 600 yards to a gate and the B3135. Turn around and retrace your steps back through Black Rock to the gate on the right that gives access to

Velvet Bottom. Walk back up through Velvet Bottom to a gate and road at its far end, turn right and, in 25 yards, left through a handgate back into that area of 'gruffy ground'. Follow the path ahead back to the road leading into the parking area. Turn right back to the car park at the site of the former **Blackmoor lead workings**.

Reminders of the mine workings that took place here.

Hinton Blewett and Chewton Wood

Fine views are a feature of this walk.

A **walking friend has this theory** that many a good circular walk is missed because it straddles two adjoining maps. This walk is a case in point, stretching as it does across the pair of OS Explorer sheets that

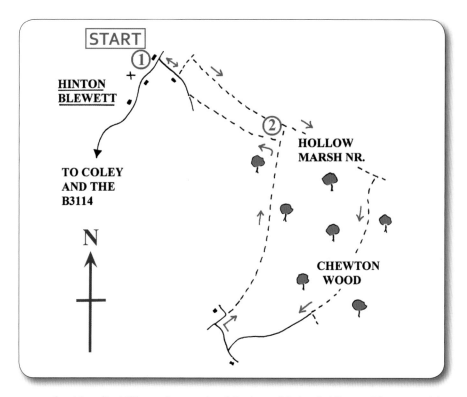

cover the Mendip Hills to the south of Bath and Bristol. Hinton Blewett, with its hilltop location, is a picturesque village where the church, pub and some older houses overlook a pleasant village green, known for whatever reason as 'Barbury'. From the village, a fieldpath with views is followed gently downhill to Hollow Marsh Nature Reserve – with its wetland flora and fauna – before the walk passes through the extensive tree cover of Chewton Wood. Beyond this area of mixed woodland, an ancient green lane known as 'Hollow Marsh Lane' returns the walk to Hinton Blewett, completing a secluded and little walked corner of the Eastern Mendip Hills.

Dogs will enjoy running free across the fields at the start of the walk, as well as retrieving sticks in the vast expanse of Chewton Wood. They will also enjoy the enclosed green lane that runs back to Hinton Blewett at journey's end, with all sorts of noises and smells in the hedgerows that border this ancient track.

Terrain

Decent fieldpaths, byways and tracks that cross an occasionally hilly landscape.

Dog factors

Distance: 5 miles.
Road walking: Short sections of road walking at Hinton Blewett and virtually traffic-free lanes between Chewton Wood and Hollow Marsh Lane.
Livestock: Cattle are occasionally to be found grazing in one of the fields between Hinton Blewett and Chewton Wood.
Livestock: None.
Stiles: 2 stiles that are easy to negotiate for all but the largest of dogs. An alternative shorter walk is suggested for the likes of Bernese mountain dogs and very elderly labradors!
Nearest vets: Silva House Veterinary Group in Midsomer Norton. ☎ 01761 412223.

Where to park

The parking area by the green opposite the Ring O' Bells Inn at Hinton Blewett (GR ST 595569). **OS maps:** Explorers 141 Cheddar Gorge & Mendip Hills West and 142 Shepton Mallet & Mendip Hills East.

How to get there

The B3114 runs between the A39 at Chewton Mendip and the A368 at West Harptree. Leave the B3114 at Coley, midway between these two villages, and follow a network of signposted lanes up into Hinton Blewett.

Nearest refreshments

The walk starts/finishes by the Ring O' Bells in Hinton Blewett. This is an archetypal village green pub that is – to quote from its website – 'idyllically located betwixt the Mendip Hills and the beautiful Chew Valley'. The blurb continues: 'drinkers, diners, families, walkers and cyclists all welcome ... and anyone else'. It is owned by Somerset's Butcombe Brewery, so be sure to sample one of their fine real ales as you rest and linger in the courtyard garden with your dog. ☎ 01761 451245.

The Walk

1 Follow the road below the **Ring O' Bells**, signposted to Litton and Chewton

Lisa in Chewton Wood.

Mendip. In 150 yards, with the village hall on the right, pass through a gateway on the left and follow the waymarked Limestone Link across a field to a gate opposite. Beyond this gate, turn right and walk up the side of the field, keeping ahead where the hedge ends to reach a gate in the opposite field boundary. Cross the next field to a gate opposite before walking down the right edge of the next field to a point where the hedge and path bear right to a gateway. In the next field, bear half-left, dropping downhill to cross a stream in a shallow valley, before climbing uphill to a gate in the top left corner of the field ahead. Walk down the right edge of the next field, pass through a gap on the right in its bottom corner and turn immediately left to pass through a gateway. Immediately, turn right through a gap in the hedge before turning left to walk downhill to a gate at the bottom of the field (*).

2 Follow the right edge of the meadow ahead, woodland on the right, along to a stile and footbridge over a stream before crossing **Hollow Marsh Nature Reserve** to a stile and woodland. At the end of a short section of woodland path, turn left and cross a stream before turning right and walking down to a gate in the bottom right corner of the field ahead. Pass through this gateway and cross a track to a gateway opposite to follow a permissive bridleway into **Chewton Wood.** Follow the track ahead through the woodland for ½ mile to a gate and a lane, keeping ahead at all junctions in the woodland. Follow the lane ahead for ½ mile to a junction, turn right and, at the next junction in 350 yards, turn right again. In 25 yards, where the road bears left, veer right onto a bridleway. Follow this track for just over 1 mile to a junction by some woodland, turn left and follow a track for ¾ mile to a road on the edge of **Hinton Blewett**. Turn right and, in 350 yards, the walk returns to the **Ring O' Bells**.

(*) **NOTE** for larger and older dogs that cannot negotiate stiles. On reaching the end of point 1, turn right to the corner of the field, pass through a gate and follow the track ahead for 25 yards to a junction. Follow the track to the left – **Hollow Marsh Lane** – for ¾ mile to a road. Retrace your steps to that junction, turn left and follow a track for ¾ mile to a road on the edge of **Hinton Blewett**. Follow this road to the right back to the **Ring O' Bells**.

Chew Magna and Chew Valley Lake

Chew Valley Lake.

Just a few miles south of Bristol lies the Chew Valley, as popular with commuters today as it was with the Bronze Age settlers who built the noted stone circle at Stanton Drew many hundreds of years BC. The valley is bounded to the north by Dundry Hill and to the south by the Mendip Hills, and contains Chew Valley Lake, a reservoir that was formed in 1956 following the construction of a dam across the River Chew. Its statistics are daunting – a 500-yard-long dam, a lake 2½ miles in length and a capacity of some 4,500 million gallons.

Chew Magna, described as a 'praty cloathing toun' by Leland, Henry VIII's antiquary, has long since lost its industrial connections. The fine Georgian houses alongside the raised pavement tell of Chew's later prosperity when it became home to many of Bristol's more affluent and professional people. Certain to catch the eye are St Andrew's church with its fine tower and fine old preaching cross, Chew Court, at one time the Palace of the Bishop of Bath and Wells, and the 15th-century Old School Room.

Dogs will love the open spaces of Knowle Hill, with views extending across the Chew Valley, as well as the riverside path alongside the Chew. With sticks everywhere, dogs who enjoy a swim will be in and out of the water all of the time on this part of the walk.

Terrain

Well-defined paths; a moderate climb onto Knowle Hill.

Where to park

The free public car park alongside the Pelican Inn at Chew Magna (GR ST 575631). **OS map:** Explorer 155 Bristol & Bath.

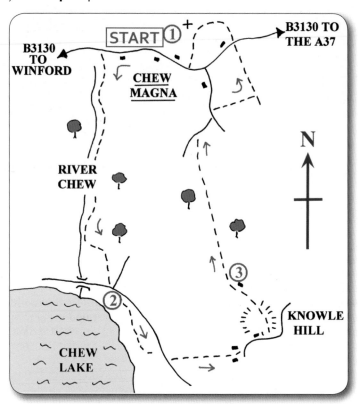

Chew Magna and Chew Valley Lake (18)

How to get there

Chew Magna lies on the B3130, which links the A37 with the A38 south of Bristol. The Pelican Inn is in the heart of the village on the High Street, opposite the church.

Nearest refreshments

The Pelican Inn, with its intriguing 'Pelly Plank' dishes, lies literally at journey's end. Whilst the inn has more of a restaurant feel, there is an excellent garden that is very welcoming to dogs who, incidentally, would relish a packet of the Pelican's genuine Black Country pork scratchings. ☎ 01275 331777. There is also an excellent café at Chew Valley Lake with a patio area suitable for dogs.

Dog factors

Distance: 3½ miles.
Road walking: A short section of pavement walking in Chew Magna at the start.
Livestock: Cattle are occasionally to be found grazing in one of the fields between Hinton Blewett and Chewton Wood.
Livestock: Occasionally in the fields by the River Chew.
Stiles: A very low stile at the entrance to Chew Magna church.
Nearest vets: Golden Valley Vets in Chew Magna.
☎ 01275 332442.

The Walk

1 Exit the car park and follow the B3130 to the left for 300 yards. Immediately before a property numbered 26, turn left down a footpath to reach a bridge over the **River Chew**. Turn left, cross the river and continue along to another footbridge. Beyond this bridge, turn right along towards a property called **Dumpers Cottage**. Just before this property, pass through a gateway on the left into an open field. Turn to the right and walk across five fields, the River Chew to the right all the while. On the far side of the fifth field, pass through a gateway and walk through a copse to join an access road leading down to a waterworks complex on the right. Follow this access road uphill to the left and, in 250 yards, just before a gate and road, turn right and walk along the

What's Finn found?

top edge of the field down to a gate in the corner of the field. Join the road running from Chew Stoke to Bishop Sutton, turn left and then take the second of two entrances into the **Chew Valley Lake picnic area**.

2 Immediately past a car parking pay hut, turn left and join a gravelled path that runs along the side of Chew Valley Lake. Follow this path for 500 yards through to another parking area. Towards the far end of this car park, turn left and follow an access road up to a road, turn right and, in 50 yards, pass through a handgate on the left and follow a path up the left edges of two fields. Beyond the second field, follow the left edge of a lawn up to a handgate on the left, walk ahead into a gravelled parking area by **Denny Barn** and turn right up to a road. Turn left and follow the road around the southern edge of **Knowle Hill**, an area of common land. Having passed a drive on the right leading to a farm, continue for 100 yards to a path on the left that heads uphill through the bracken-strewn slopes of Knowle Hill. Ignoring any side turns, continue across the hillside for 250 yards to a T-junction. Turn left and continue to a junction on the western edge of Knowle Hill. Follow the path to the right across the edge of the common to its north-western corner before continuing down an enclosed path bordering a property on the right to a gate and open field.

3 Walk down the right edge of this field to pick up a gravelled track by a property on the right. Follow this track for just over ½ mile down to its junction with **Denny Lane**. Turn right and, at a junction in 100 yards, turn left and, in another 100 yards, pass through a gateway on the right opposite **Coach House** into an open field. Follow a path ahead across four fields before dropping down some steps at the far side of the fourth field to join an enclosed path. Follow this path to the left, cross a footbridge over the **River Chew** and cross one final field to join the B3130 on the edge of **Chew Magna**. Follow the driveway opposite up to Chew Court before passing to the right of this property to continue along to a stile and **Chew Magna church**. Walk through the churchyard to the B3130 – opposite is the **Pelican Inn**, to the right of which is the car park.

Chew Valley Lake seen from Knowle Hill.

Bradford-on-Avon and Avoncliff

The magnificent tithe barn near the canal.

Bradford-on-Avon has been described as 'Bath in miniature', with its ranks of handsome stone cottages lining the hillside about the River Avon. The town's prosperity was founded upon the wool trade in centuries past, evidence of which is all around in the fine merchants' houses and imposing mills; grand structures that have since been converted into desirable flats and apartments. One of England's finest small towns, Bradford

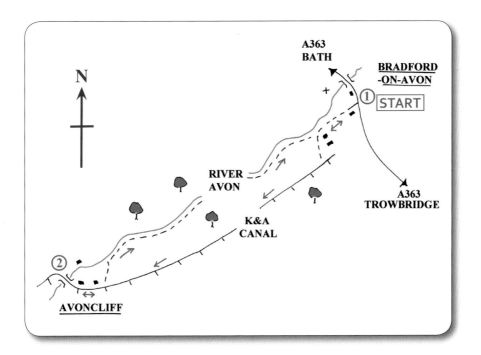

can also boast an ancient tithe barn, a Saxon church and a diminutive lock-up on the handsome Town Bridge.

The Kennet & Avon Canal and the River Avon both run between Bradford-on-Avon and neighbouring Avoncliff, a tiny hamlet deep in the Avon Valley where a vast aqueduct carries the canal across the river. The walk follows the canal towpath to Avoncliff, before returning through the meadows that border the River Avon. It is not difficult to see why this walk is one of the most popular excursions in the region, with its waterside paths, the fine architecture and the beautiful setting within the boundaries of what is known as Barton Farm Country Park.

Dogs will love what is essentially a traffic-free walk, as well as the company of many other dogs for whom this is a favourite destination. They will enjoy running free in the meadows alongside the Avon, as well as enjoying a splash in the river in Bradford at journey's end alongside a centuries-old packhorse bridge.

Terrain

A flat walk, with the exception of a flight of steps that drop down to the river from the canal.

Bristol & Bath – A Dog Walker's Guide

Dog factors

Distance: 3 miles.
Road walking: None – but keep your dog under control in the station car park.
Stiles: None.
Livestock: None.
Nearest vets: Harris, Hill & Gibbons in Bradford-on-Avon.
☎ 01225 862656.

Where to park

The station car park in Bradford-on-Avon (GR ST 825606). **OS map:** Explorer 156 Chippenham & Bradford-on-Avon.

How to get there

Follow the A4 eastwards from Bath to Bathford before turning onto the A363 road signposted to Bradford-on-Avon. In the centre of the town, cross the Town Bridge and, at a mini roundabout in 100 yards, turn right into station car park.

Nearest refreshments

The Cross Guns at Avoncliff, at the halfway point on the walk, is quite the perfect place to rest and linger awhile. Dating from the 17th century, this was the watering hole of local weavers long before the K&A canal turned the inn into a bargees' pub in the late 18th century. On the terrace that drops down to the Avon are any number of picnic tables overlooking the river. Dogs will enjoy lazing here whilst their owners can enjoy the fine food and real ales – from the nearby Box Steam Brewery – for which the Cross Guns is so well known. ☎ 01225 862335.

The Walk

1 Walk to the far end of the station car park and follow a path that drops down to the left to pass under a railway bridge, the River Avon on the right. Continue on a path that crosses a grassy recreation area to a junction of paths, a packhorse bridge on the right. Follow the path ahead, still bordering the River Avon, for a few paces before turning left to cross an area of open grassland to the right of the Barton Farm complex of buildings. On the far side of the open grassland, follow a stepped path up to the Kennet & Avon Canal. Turn right and follow the towpath for 1¼ miles into Avoncliff.

2 Having enjoyed the delights of the Cross Guns, follow the towpath back towards Bradford-on-Avon and, in 100 yards, just past the last property on the left, follow a stepped path on the left down to meadowland by the River Avon. Follow the river to the right upstream for ¾ mile across three fields to a gate on the far side of the third field. Beyond this gate, continue along a path alongside the Avon to reach a tarmac riverside path. Follow this path back to the Barton Farm complex of buildings by the packhorse bridge passed at the outset. Retrace your steps across the grassy recreation area and under the railway bridge before bearing right back up to the station car park.

Bradford-on-Avon's wonderful Saxon church.

The popular pub at Avoncliff, the halfway point of the walk.

Monkton Combe and Midford

The tranquil Tucking Mill Reservoir.

The village of **Monkton Combe** is best known for its public school, a religious foundation established by the Reverend Francis Pocock in 1868. From the centre of the village, the walk follows a very quiet lane through to Tucking Mill, a diminutive hamlet where a delightful reservoir, an imposing railway viaduct on the former Somerset & Dorset Railway and William Smith's cottage will all catch the eye. Smith was immortalised in Simon Winchester's book *The Map That Changed the World*, the map in question being the world's first geological map, which was published in 1815. Smith was resident in Tucking Mill whilst working as Chief Engineer on the nearby Somerset Coal Canal, where the discovery of a section of rock strata was the inspiration for the map. The trackbed of the S&D Railway, a victim of the 1960s Beeching cuts, is followed through to Midford, before a delightful riverside path alongside the Midford Brook marks the return to Monkton Combe.

Dogs will thoroughly enjoy the section of railway path with its absence of traffic, stiles and livestock, whilst the riverside section will prove alluring to any dogs who simple love splashing around in water. There is one short section of busy road along the B3110 in Midford where dogs will need to be kept on a tight rein, but otherwise this is a perfect walk for man's best friend.

Terrain

Well-defined field paths and tracks that cross a gently undulating landscape; potentially muddy by the Midford Brook following heavy rain.

Where to park

The free public car park opposite Monkton Combe church (GR ST 773620). **OS map:** Explorer 155 Bristol & Bath.

How to get there

Heading south out of Bath, leave the A36 at the traffic lights on the edge of Monkton Combe some 6 miles from the city, turning right onto the foot of Brassknocker Hill. In 75 yards, take the left turn into the centre of Monkton Combe and, on a right-hand bend by the church, turn right into the car park.

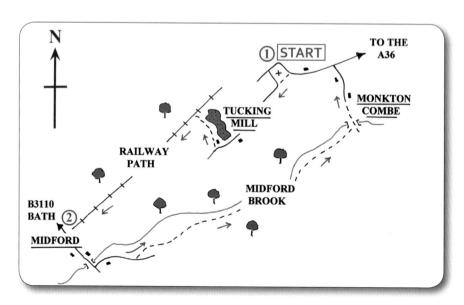

Nearest refreshments

The Wheelwrights Arms in Monkton Combe has a fine reputation for the quality of its food. Dogs therefore have to be content with the inn's garden, which is no bad place to be! ☎ 01225 722287. An alternative option is to drive back to the A36 to the nearby Brassknocker Basin and enjoy rest and refreshment at the Angelfish Restaurant whose picnic tables overlook a restored section of the Somerset Coal Canal. ☎ 01225 723483.

The Walk

1 Leave the car park, turn left for a few paces and then right to walk past **Monkton Combe church** to a gate in the end churchyard wall. Beyond this gate, follow a lane around a bend on the left through to **Tucking Mill**. Having passed the entrance to **Tucking Mill Reservoir** and then **Tucking Mill Cottage** on the right, turn right onto a footpath that runs alongside the former home of William Smith to reach a tarmac road alongside the reservoir. Follow this ahead for 50 yards before climbing some steps on the left up to the trackbed of the former S&D Railway. Follow the trackbed to the left for ½ mile to the car park of the **Hope & Anchor** in **Midford** before dropping down to the B3110.

2 Turn left and, in 200 yards, turn left into **Midford Lane**. In 300 yards, pass through the second of two gates on the left and follow the left edges of three fields. On the far side of the third field, keep on the path as it drops

Dog factors

Distance: 3 miles.
Road walking: A short section of quiet lane between Monkton Combe and Midford; 100 yards of pavement on the busy B3110 in Midford itself.
Livestock: Cattle are occasionally to be found grazing in one of the fields between Midford and Monkton Combe on the return leg of the walk.
Stiles: None.
Nearest vets: 24/7 Rosemary Lodge Veterinary Hospital in Wellsway, Bath. ☎ 01225 832521.

The site of the former Midford railway station.

down to pass through a small area of woodland. Beyond a handgate, follow a wooden causeway to another gate before crossing the next field on a path that subsequently drops down to join the banks of the **Midford Brook**. Keep ahead to a gate and continue following the riverbank for 350 yards to a gate and junction. Turn left, crossing a wooden bridge before continuing along an enclosed path that joins **Mill Lane** in **Monkton Combe**. Follow this road ahead back to a junction in the centre of the village and turn left to return to the car park by the church.